NEVER LET GO!

By

Linda Paul-Graham

Cover Illustrated by Linda Paul-Graham

Proof-reading by

Wordsmith Editing

&

Aaron Graham

Dedicated to

Ann

My mentor and friend

Haverton Hill

"For You formed my inward parts;
You covered me in my mother's
womb. I will praise You, for I am
fearfully and wonderfully made."
Psalms 139: 13 -14

 Some of the earliest and happiest
memories I have is of my home in
Haverton Hill, North East England. A
home I shared with Mam, Dad and my
elder sister Angela. Haverton Hill was too
large to be a village but too small to be
called a town. It was a close-knit
community, everyone seemed friendly and
would always say 'hello' and smile when
passing.

At the end of our street lay open fields,
golden with wheat in the summer months.
Amongst these fields lay a beck where

many a happy hour was had paddling in its cool waters. Beside the fields was the 'bendy'. I've no idea why it was called that; it was a small playground containing a set of swings, a round-a-bout, and a very old and stiff see-saw.

Our humble home was a council-owned semi- detached house. We shared a front gate and entryway, a kind of tunnel that linked two houses together and led to the back gardens. Norman, our neighbour on the left hand side was the local postman. Our neighbour on the right was a lovely old lady called Mrs Ventress, who loved to chat to Mam across the back garden fence. Three large steps with a low wall on either side led to our front door, No. 47. On either side of the steps were Mam's lovely Red Hot Pokers; their tall green stems with red and yellow spiky flowers waving in the breeze. In those days people only used the front door on special occasions. The back door was flanked on one side by the coal house and on the other by the toilet. opened directly into the kitchen with it's brick red walls that Dad had decorated with paint acquired from the shipyard where he worked. Directly opposite the back door was a large window which looked out on to the front garden. In the corner beside the window, was a large built in cupboard called 'the pantry'. Opposite the pantry was the large stone sink, where I washed my hands after a morning spent making mud pies or, as I called it, 'sloppy molly'. A gas cooker, a kitchen cabinet, and a table with four chairs round it were the only other items of furniture in the kitchen. Well-worn lino covered the floor. On the left leading from the kitchen was the living room. At the time, this seemed to me, a very large room. It had two wide windows, one looking out on to the front garden and the other onto the back. Bright blue, red and yellow squares patterned the lino covered floor. These squares provided us with endless entertainment during long winter days as we made up games, such as Angela could only step on the red squares and I the blue. We would turn the fireguard (slightly triangular in shape) upside down and use it as a boat sailing on the sea. Or we would drape sheets over the clothes horse and make a tent. The room was furnished with a red three-piece suite, a china cabinet, and a sideboard. To the left of the fireplace was a huge floor-to-ceiling built-in cupboard. A small rug lay in front of the fire. Leading from the living room was a very small lobby where the stairs and the front door were. The stairs were painted white at the sides with bare wood in the middle. At the top of the stairs, to the left was Mam and Dad's bedroom, somewhere we only entered when invited. Straight ahead was the bathroom, containing an enormous claw-footed, metal bath, a wash basin, and a medicine cabinet. Next to the bathroom and at the back of the house, was the spare room. Numerous bags and boxes were stored here along with various toys. Our dolls "Guggles" and "Looby Loo" lived here. At the front of the house, on the right-hand side of the stairs was my room, which I shared with my big sister, Angela. It was decorated with Pinky and Perky wallpaper. Angela said the red pig was hers so that made the blue pig mine! To the left of the door were our single beds with a rug in between them. The room had a high window with a wide sill, and if we stood on my bed we could manage to climb and sit on it. Looking out of this window, we could see between the rooftops of the houses opposite to distant fields where horses were kept. Two sets of drawers completed the furniture for this room. The house did not have central heating; the coal fire downstairs was the sole source of warmth. As a result, the bedrooms were freezing cold in the winter months. Mam would put her old coats on our beds and fill hot water bottles to give us extra warmth. At bedtime there would be a battle: Angela didn't like the dark and would want the light on. I couldn't sleep with the light on. So each night we argued. Mam resolved the situation by leaving the landing light on and the door open. Angela and I would snuggle under the covers, chatting away to each other

"what you gonna dream about tonight,

Linda? "Angela would ask.

"I dunno "I replied sleepily.

"I do", says she.

I'm going to dream about a red car",
declared Angela.

Determined to dream the same I would
drop off to sleep.

I think I must have been around four years
old when Angela started school and I was
left to spend my days playing at home. I
made the most of the opportunity by
playing with all of Angela's toys which,
normally, she wouldn't allow me to play
with. My favourite was Angela's Tiny
Tears doll because when you fed it with a
bottle of water it cried and wet itself.
Angela looked after her toys; they always
seemed to be as new as the day she got
them. Her dolls wore lovely dresses and
all were kept neat and tidy. On the other
hand, my dolls were scribbled on, the hair
was cut, fingers bitten off, and the eyes
poked out. I broke an arm off my Tiny
Tears within a short while of getting it.
Once I got a 'Chatty Cathy' for Christmas.

Pulling a cord in her back made her talk. She spoke about ten different phrases, including;

"Hi, My name is Chatty Cathy",

or

"I love you"

After only a few days I snapped the cord. Dad was annoyed. In an attempt to fix Chatty Cathy, he sawed her in half to get at the cord inside her, but to no avail. Chatty Cathy was left with a permanent bandage of strong masking tape round her middle. It was so much more fun playing with Angela's toys, but no matter how I tried to hide the evidence Angela always knew I had been using her things. On fine days I would sit in the back garden and make mud pies (sloppy molly), or I would go to the little place just behind the garden shed where I would force Michael, a friend from two doors down, to play 'house'. The back wall of the shed made the perfect fireplace, (because it had a small hollow shape at its base), where we would pretend to cook our mud pies. On summer evenings and weekends I would 'help' Dad with the gardening. In the front garden he planted potatoes or sometimes spinach. Turnips and coriander (dhanya Dad called it), were grown in the back garden. We had a rhubarb plant from which Mam would give me a stalk. I would be given a bowl of sugar and would sit happily on the back step, dipping the stalk in the sugar, enjoying my treat.

The following year it was my turn to join Angela at school. I was eager to go. I wanted to be a school girl like Angela. That first morning, I left Mam's side without a backward glance. In the cloakroom I hung my coat on the peg with my picture on it as I'd seen Angela do so many times before, waved goodbye to Mam and followed the teacher into the classroom. The school day began with assembly. We sang songs called hymns and read a story from a book, the teacher referred to as The Bible. We were asked to put our hands together and close our eyes whilst someone talked to God, this was called prayer. Two or three times a year I had the honour of choosing a hymn and a prayer for that Assembly. I chose the same ones each time; the teachers must have been fed up. We would choose the prayer from a large flip book. My favourite had a picture of lambs skipping about. To match this I chose the hymn 'Loving Shepherd of Thy Sheep' (number 366 in Songs of Praise) which goes as follows:

Loving Shepherd of thy sheep,
Keep thy lamb, in safety keep;
Nothing can thy power with-stand,
Non can pluck me from thy hand
I would bless thee every day,
Gladly all thy will obey,
Like thy blessed ones above
Happy in thy precious love.

Loving Shepherd, ever near,
Teach thy lamb thy voice to hear;
Suffer not my steps to stray
From the straight and narrow way.

Where thou leadest I would go,
Walking in thy steps below,
Till before my Father's throne
I shall know as I am known.

During the morning lessons, I discovered the magic of books and stories. I loved reading so much I would save up my pocket money and buy little story books instead of sweets. In scripture lessons we were told stories such as Jesus entering Jerusalem on Palm Sunday, of when Zechariah was struck dumb, and when baby Jesus was born. We had to re-tell the stories in our work books and could draw pictures to accompany them which I loved to do. I gave Joseph a red tunic with a purple sash and purple robe, whilst Mary would be clothed in blue. As much as I enjoyed scripture lessons, I disliked maths and P.E.; even when we got to use Pogo sticks. Mid-morning we were given milk to drink which arrived in small glass bottles. As milk monitor we got to put a straw in each of the bottles. In winter ice would form on the top, whilst in summer it was disgustingly warm. In the afternoon we got to play with toys. My favourite was the Wendy House, with it's miniature furniture, pots and pans. Some days we would have music time. All classes would gather in the hall. Sitting crossed legged on oval shaped, rush mats, we learnt new songs, with lines like, "hens go cluck cluck, cows go moo moo, fiddly hi dee, fiddly hi dee"

My Parents

*He will cover you with His feathers, and
under His wings you will find refuge"
Psalm 91:4*

Dad was from West Bengal in India; he
worked his passage aboard a ship and
came to the UK. His name was
Chittaranjan Paul, but everyone just called
him Paul. On the other hand, Mam was
born in a place a little less exotic. She was
born and brought up in Middlesbrough.
She had two brothers and four sisters.
Mam's childhood was not always a happy
one; her father was violent and she
suffered abuse at his hands. Mam was
introduced to my Dad by her eldest sister,
she was in her early teens. Dad was 27
and Mam only 16 when they married.
Angela was born three years later and I
eighteen months after that.
The early years of their marriage were
spent living in various rented rooms in the

Teesside area until they finally settled in Haverton Hill. Dad worked in the shipyard on the River Tees. If a ship from India came into the docks Dad would make friends with the crew and, sometimes, they would come back to our house. We were allowed to stay up on those occasions. We would have fiery curry followed by mangoes (from the ship), rice and evaporated milk. Sometimes Dad would take me with him to visit friends on the ship. I would climb the big steps at the side of the huge hulk to be lifted over the doorway in to its dark corridors. The interior smelt of oil and spices. The crew dressed casually in lunghi's (traditional Indian dress consisting of a piece of cloth wrapped around the waist) walked by smiling at me and pinching my cheek. We would be taken to one of the cabins and given food which included very spicy curry and always tinned pineapple rings and evaporated milk. A great fuss was made of me, as I reminded the men of the families they'd left behind.

Every now and then Mam would take us on the bus to Port Clarence, about 2 miles away, situated on the North Bank of the River Tees. We rode across the river on the Transporter Bridge, an iconic structure. At the bottom it had a kind of platform. Cars would drive into the middle of this platform whilst at the two sides, foot passengers stood in covered shelters. The bridge moved the platform over the water until we reached the South Bank. Another five minute bus journey took us to Nana's house. I loved visiting Nana and playing with my cousins. Nana had a dark brown sideboard in her living room and we would while away the time rummaging through its drawers and cupboards. Often, we would find old copies of the Bunty or other comics to read. Bunty was a favourite because it had paper dolls that you could cut out and dress. If it was fine, we would play in Nana's back garden where there was a big mound (Nana said it was the old air raid shelter) over which a big lilac tree draped its branches. It smelt wonderful in the spring. We played all sorts of make believe games on that mound, as well as king of the castle. As I got older, I would sleep over for the odd few days. whilst there I would play with my cousins and run errands for Nana.

Occasionally Margaret, a teenage girl from down our street, would come to our house to babysit us. On those occasions Mam would put her hair up in a beehive and dress up in her mini skirt and tall white boots. Other times we would visit Dad's Indian friends. The men gathered in one room to drank beer and talk, whilst the women prepared food and chatted amongst themselves in another. It was lovely to see all the colourful saris.

A certain etiquette was followed when serving the meal. Courses were served, vegetables and dhal first, followed by fish, then meat or chicken curry. These were accompanied by boiled rice, chapatis and a variety of chutneys. Dessert was either Indian rice pudding, thick, creamy and flavoured with bay leaves and sultanas, or Indian sweets, usually cooked by Dad.

Children were served first, then the men and lastly the women ate.

One day, when I was six years old I returned home after having spent a good few hours playing out, to find Mam sitting listlessly in her chair. She asked if I would fetch 'Aunty Irene'. A few really good friends and neighbours were always referred to as Aunty. There was Aunty Irene, Aunty Margaret, Aunty Nora, and Aunty Barbara. Aunty Irene lived next door but one, the other side of Norman the postman. After fetching Aunty Irene, Mam was taken to hospital and I spent the rest of the day at Aunty Margaret's. I played with their Spaniel, Ricky, and had my first taste of rum and raisin ice cream. It was here Dad found me when he returned from work and took me home.

Brownies

"I promise that
I shall do my best
To do my duty to God
To serve the Queen and
Help other people,
and keep the
Brownie Guide Law"

When I was seven my friend Michael (Irene's son) started going to Cubs. I was asked if I would like to go to Brownies. I didn't know what it was but I liked the idea of an outing, so I said yes. We got the bus to Billingham, the nearest town to us, which had a shopping centre, and walked to a nearby church building. Inside were lots of girls about my age in brown uniforms and a couple of ladies in blue uniforms. Around the outside of the Church hall, trestle tables had been set up and there was what looked like glue, scissors, and various craft materials on them. In the centre of the room stood a large red and white toadstool. Everyone gathered round the toadstool and sang a song. They made a funny sign with their hands, thumb folded into the palm, holding the pinky finger down, whilst the three remaining fingers remained straight. I later learned this was the Brownie Salute. I had a lovely evening playing games and making things. At the end I was given the Brownie Promise and the Brownie Guide Law to take home and learn.

After I had been going to Brownies for some time Michael's family asked if I'd like to go with him to Sunday School too. I absolutely *loved* Sunday School. We listened to stories, sang songs, and coloured in pictures which we could take home. If Michael couldn't make it to Sunday School, I would put on my favourite white dress, get the bus to Billingham, and go all by myself. One time at Sunday School I was presented with a Children's Bible. It had interesting stories accompanied by beautiful pictures in it. I absolutely loved it!

Billingham

*"The name of the Lord is a
strong tower: the righteous run into it,
and are safe"*
                    Proverbs 18:10

In September 1971 my sister Mandy was
born. After eight years I was no longer the
baby of the family; it was great! I loved
playing with Mandy, much better than a
doll. I spent what seemed like hours
singing every lullaby I knew; it's amazing
she has turned out so musical, as I'm tone
deaf.

About a year later, with great sadness we
left our home in Haverton Hill. The
council were demolishing the whole
village as it was right in the middle of the
chemical works and deemed unfit. We
moved to another council house in South
Billingham. It was a newly built house,
the garden still unfinished with a great big
step down from the back door. The garden

was just soil with bricks strewn about, no grass. We could not wallpaper because the plaster had to dry out. At the end of the street was the entrance to the chemical works.

The move meant starting a new school. For the first time I had a male teacher. In my previous school I'd just started learning long division; here they were teaching area, volume and 'simple' algebra. I was completely out of my depth. To make matters worse I was seated in front of a most obnoxious boy who constantly called me names such as blacky, nigger, and packi. In fact, racism and bullying followed me through-out the school. I was so unhappy and dreaded going. I found a small amount of respite in the sewing class.

In assembly it was announced there was to be a country dance class starting. I'd seen the dancers at Billingham International Folklore Festival and quite fancied having a go. The meeting was at lunchtime; normally I would go home, but that day I took a packed lunch. Pushing open the doors to the main hall, I crept in.

Everyone was standing in a circle; a male teacher with a very large tummy and a loud voice stood in the centre. To my horror each person had to sing a few scales. I croaked out a few notes thinking it a strange requirement for country dancing. Later I discovered I'd gone to the wrong venue and I had attended the audition for the school choir; needless to say, I didn't get in!

The racism wasn't confined to school. Neighbours' refused to talk to my family except to call names or shout abuse. There was one exception, a neighbour who had two daughters, Laura and Sarah, the same ages as Angela and I. They were very creative, all the family played musical instruments. Laura and Sarah enjoyed baking and needlework. It is from them we learnt to crochet. Angela and I would save our money, go to the wool shop, and buy hanks of wool from the bargain basket. Once home, we took turns (though it was usually me) to hold the hank between two hands held up, whilst the other wound it into a ball. If no one was available to hold the hank I'd stretch it across the back of a dining chair. Our home gradually filled with crocheted cushion covers and blankets. In addition to crochcting we learnt how to bake basic sponge cakes.

Even though we lived nearer, I stopped going to Sunday School, and I joined a different Brownie group. It wasn't the same. Everyone had their own little groups of friends and I didn't fit in. I did, however, discover the library, a place where you could borrow books for free! Up until now I did not know such places existed. I became a regular visitor, immersing myself in the world of story books.

For some reason, Billingham was a place where I spent the most time with Dad. We would go on outings together, just the two of us. Often, we went to the old Billy Baths, as we both enjoyed swimming, Angela wasn't so keen. Dad used to take us both to the more modern pool at the Forum in Billingham Town Centre. We had great fun splashing around with our swim rings on. The Billy Baths were old.

The walls tiled cream and a dark green. The changing cubicles were wooden with paint peeling off them, but I loved it there. Sometimes Dad would give me a piggy back and swim to the deep end. On one occasion he was told not to do this and I had to stay at the shallow end. The attendant observed me, said I was being lazy and could probably swim without the ring. He gave me a few lessons where I would try swimming the width of the pool with- out my ring. I made a few attempts but felt safer with my swim ring.

On another occasion I was taken to the shipyard were Dad worked. We had a little chat with his work colleagues then returned home, complete with little black kitten in a shoe box. I later named him Sooty.

Then came a very special outing. Dad took me to London. Angela had been taken when she was five so it was deemed my turn. We travelled by National Coach, the trip taking over five hours. Stopping at a motorway station for lunch I chose a large plate of fish chips and peas (though I didn't care for garden peas). I eagerly shook salt and vinegar on, then tucked in. Urrgh, it tasted awful! I'd mistaken the sugar shaker (I'd not seen one before) for the salt pot.

We stayed with Uncle Bose and his family. Uncle Bose had been best man at my parents' wedding; that's about all I know about him. The next few days were spent in a whirlwind tour of London. Feeding pigeons at Trafalgar Square followed by a very long walk to Buckingham Palace. Then lunch in St James Park, feeding the ducks and swans. We had a trip to Windsor on an open top bus and walked round the castle. Here there was a display of a doll-house, but we didn't see that as you had to pay. We sat by the river for lunch; it was a scorching hot day, so we rested watching sailing vessels on the river. On the way back to the bus stop I bought a guard doll with his bright red uniform and bearskin hat as a souvenir. Next day we visited Regents Park Zoo. We saw elephants, fierce tigers, creepy snakes and the pandas Cha Cha and Chi Chi; although they were asleep.

I'd been to Flamingo Land Zoo with the school, but this was on a different scale with a greater variety of animals. All too soon it was time to return home. A few weeks later Uncle Bose and his family came to stay with us. The whole family of five, crammed into our small spare room.

We lived in Billingham for little over a year. The situation at school and with our neighbours hadn't improved and we were all deeply unhappy. Angela and I were told Dad had bought our very own house; it was across the river, nearer to his work, Indian friends and Mam's family.

Warwick Street

"If any one would come after me, let him deny himself and take up his cross and follow me"

Matt 16:24

Moving day arrived. I was so excited, but also a bit miffed. Angela had gone to help clean the new house, which meant she saw it before me. As a consolation, I travelled in the removal van with all the furniture which was much more interesting. The van pulled into a long narrow street with houses on either side. The doors of these houses opened right on to the street; there was no garden. A road ran across the street two thirds of the way down dividing it into two. A corner shop was situated at the intersection of the road and street. Our house was right in the middle of the lower part of the street. The front door had a white painted frame with frosted glass in the middle. Behind the frosted glass was some black cast iron worked into a scrolling pattern with leaves on it. To the side of the door was a sash window with another one above it on the second floor. We entered a tiny square hall/porch, (big enough for two people at the most) and went through a second door into the living room. To the right was a gas fire with a stone surround. On the wall opposite the hall door were a further two doors: one directly opposite the hall, and one in the corner near the fireplace. Entering the first door I passed by a cupboard under the stairs into a long, narrow kitchen. Although the kitchen had two largish windows, it seemed gloomy as it was painted a very dark blue. In the kitchen would go our dining table, chairs, Formica cabinet and cooker. Mandy's large Silver Cross pram was kept at the far end. At this end of the kitchen was a door leading to our only toilet, but at least it was inside. Adjacent to the toilet, a door opened onto a walled yard. The yard was bare except for a washing line, a dustbin, and Dad's bike. The yard was long and narrow. Opposite the kitchen window was a long, six foot high brick wall which separated our yard from the neighbours'. Our house

and this dividing wall formed the length
of the yard. A narrower wall with a gate
set in it joined the two together. The gate
led into a long tiled alley which ran the
length of the block of houses.

The door in the corner of the living room
led to the staircase, steep and dark. A
small landing at the top branched into two
corridors. Turning left took you into the
bathroom. Further on, through the
bathroom, was a small single bedroom
with a window that looked out on to the
kitchen roof. This room was to become
Angela's. If the bathroom was occupied,
she could not enter or leave her room.
Turning right off the small landing, up
another two small steps was my bedroom.
To my disappointment it had a double bed
in it. I informed that when Mandy was old
enough I would be sharing it with her. I
did, however, get to decorate it myself. I
chose purple paint and stuck up posters of
Donny Osmond! Unlike the newly built
house in Billingham, there was no central
heating here, and the upstairs was freezing
in winter. I didn't really like this house; it
felt cold, damp, and dark, but people were

friendly enough and we settled in nicely. Many of Dad's Asian friends lived nearby and called from time to time. I made friends with Julie, who lived across the road with her parents Ian and Jean. Although Julie was a couple of years younger we got on well. We sat in each other's porches and played with our Sindy dolls. We knitted and made clothes for them. Julie had many more toys than we had and generously shared them with us. One Christmas her brother got a red chopper bike which Julie and I were allowed to ride.

Again, Angela and I started a new school. This one was called Cromwell Road School. It was a large, brick, soot stained, two-story building, with a six foot high wall surrounding the playground. I was now in third year of the juniors and Angela in the fourth. The infants' playground was on one side of the building, separated from the juniors by an iron barred gate. The junior school was on the second floor. A set of stone steps at each end of the yard led up to two huge entrance doors. Inside the entrance doors, a wide stone staircase, flanked by tiled walls, led to the cloakrooms. The cloakrooms opened out onto the main hall where many an assembly or PE class took place. Along one side of the hall were the classrooms. Angela's was the first classroom. She was in Miss Etherington's, who soon discovered Angela's artistic talent. Angela was in her element, making displays for the board in her classroom, and soon made friends. My teacher was again a man, but this one was kind and helpful. I didn't make friends easily. I was again called names by a few. The children, although friendly enough, had formed their own little groups and I was once again the new kid. I ended up befriending the misfits of the class, those called smelly or scruffy, and even a gypsy girl who attended for a short while. Shirley, a tall and loud girl, who swore a lot, who began picking on me. She kept challenging me to fight. Coming from a small sheltered school like Haverton Hill, this was very shocking and new to me. Some girls who lived in my street said Shirley would not leave me alone unless I fought her. Eventually I agreed to fight her. We arranged to meet after school on the playing fields at the end of our street. I dressed in my oldest clothes and walked with Gillian and Eva (the girls from my street), towards the playing fields. I heard the noise before I arrived, word had got round and half the school had turned out to watch. I was so nervous; I hadn't fought before. I didn't want to be considered a coward. Heart beating rapidly, shaking from head to toe, Shirley and I circled one another a few times before diving in. We kicked, clawed, pulled each other's hair. The crowd roared in the background. Shouted advice reached my ears from time to time. Tears threatened but I refused to show them. Now I'd started I wasn't going to give in. I don't remember how the fight ended, I think it was by mutual agreement, but I walked away with my head held high. I was cheered and clapped on the back, but I didn't share the enthusiasm. I returned home in tears, telling Mam I'd been fighting but I'd won. 'Why are you crying when you won?' Mam asked, then promptly scolded me for fighting. I was crying and shaking with relief; I didn't enjoy the fight but felt I had no choice if I wanted the bullying to stop. The next day, to my amazement, Shirley acted like I was her best friend, even inviting me to her home. Not only was Shirley friendly, but the rest of the class accepted me

In the July of that summer, Angela met me outside school at home time with the news that we had a new baby sister called Beverley. I met Beverley a few weeks later. Mam, I was told had undergone an operation and was recovering. When they came home Mam still wasn't well. Beverley was beautiful; small and delicate with lots of dark hair. Angela cared for Beverley feeding, changing, and bathing her.

Due to Mam's ill health, Mandy was allowed to start nursery early. I took her and picked her up. One day whilst collecting her the teacher took me aside and asked if our family was okay. Puzzled, I replied we were. The teacher went on to explain Mandy had told them we lived in a caravan as our house had burned down!

Britain was in the middle of a heatwave. Julie and I, with Mandy in her pushchair, would go on long adventures. The playing field at the end of the street contained a set of swings and a roundabout, as well as a large area for playing football. Leading from the fields was a long straight path; it had been a railway line at some point. It was hedged on either side with bramble bushes, shrubs, and trees. We walked the whole length (about three miles) of that track over the summer, exploring every nook and cranny. We took a picnic of jam sandwiches, biscuits, and a bottle of juice, which we consumed in the dens we made along the way. Sometimes we'd take containers and pick the brambles. We returned home, tired out but happy.

New School, New Friends

*"Behold I stand at the
door and knock"*
Revelation 3:20

In September 1974, I moved to the Senior
School. I was sent to Sarah Metcalf
Comprehensive, following Angela who
had started there a year earlier. Compared
to the Juniors, it was huge! Two large
buildings, one on either side of a road,
were joined together by an overhead
covered bridge. The right-hand building
had five floors housing the Science
Department, Drama, & Art classrooms,
and on the very top floor, was the
language lab. It was a room that contained
many little cubicles with desks. Inside
each cubicle was a built-in tape recorder
used to play French or German words and
phrases. We each had a headset with a
microphone and had to repeat the various
words and phrases. The teacher at the
control desk could listen in to monitor our
progress.

The left-hand building held the main hall, used for twice-weekly assemblies, concerts, and school productions. This hall also doubled as one of the school's dining rooms. This building was built in a square around an open quadrangle. One side was a corridor with the school offices and headmaster's study, together with the maths classrooms. The opposite corridor held the library, English classrooms, and foreign language classrooms. A third corridor joined the first two together and housed the Domestic Science kitchens and sewing rooms. Along the fourth corridor were the offices of the Heads of Year. These corridors were on the first floor. The ground floor housed the woodwork and metalwork shops, as well as the gym.

Next to this right-hand building was a smaller building containing the sports hall, changing rooms, and showers on the ground floor, with music rooms upstairs.

Angela's form/registration group was in one of the woodwork shops. I was in form 102. The 1 represented the school year and 02 the number of the class/study group, so as I progressed through the school it became, 202, 302, and so on. My form teacher was Mr Harry Bent, a geography teacher and a member of the Territorial (Reservist) Army; at times it felt like we had been enlisted too! There were five form groups in my year. 202 were the only group made to line up outside our form room and wait for Mr Bent to let us into the classroom. That very first morning we lined up around the classroom and had to introduce ourselves. Beside me was a tall girl with wavy, mousy coloured hair and a kind, freckled face. Her name was Linda also! We became friends from the very start.

Harry Bent ruled with a rod of iron, or rather a metre long ruler. At some stage during my first two years something was stolen within the form group. The crimson tide slowly rose up Mr Bent's neck until he was very red in the face; always an indication to keep out of the way. For what seemed like an eternity (a couple of weeks) we were made to sit boy/girl, boy/girl. Hands had to be placed on the desk in front of us and we sat in complete silence the whole registration time (both morning and afternoon registration). This sitting in silence became a regular punishment for major offences. On one occasion I made the mistake of replying to someone. I became one of the many made to spend playtime picking up litter around the school. As far as I know no other form had such procedures.

Over the years Harry Bent became less intimidating. He organized hikes at the weekends, outside of school. Linda B and I often joined these; they were my 'summer holiday'. We started doing the Duke of Edinburgh Award Scheme which Mr Bent organized. To gain the award we had to do a certain number miles hiking, take part in community events, and generally use whatever we could for self-improvement and helping the community. By the end of my time at Sarah Metcalf, I had a great respect and affection for this formidable man.

It was Linda B who invited me along to the school's Christian Union. We played games, sang songs and studied the

scriptures. My maths teacher, Mr Stocks and the RE teacher, Mr Harris ran it between them. It was held one lunchtime per week and every Friday evening after school. We all enjoyed playing 'Sword Drill'. This involved standing in a line with our bibles (provided by the group) tucked under our arms. That was termed 'Sheath Swords'. The leader would then call "Draw Swords". We took our bibles from under our arms and held them in front of us. We waited in eager anticipation. "John Chapter 3, verse 16, Romans Chapter 6 verse 22", called the teacher. We would scurry through our bibles, in a desperate attempt to be the first to find the reference. We sang songs like, "Go Tell It on the Mountain", or "I will make you Fishers of Men". My favourites were
:

> *'Follow, follow*
> *I will follow Jesus,*
> *Anywhere, everywhere*
> *I will follow on'*

And,

'I have decided to follow Jesus, (x2
No turning back, no turning back

Tho' non go with me still I will
follow, (x2)
No turning back, no turning back!

I was encouraged to attend a church. I did
not want to go alone, so I decided to try
Linda B's church. It was a three or four-
mile walk each way. There was no money
for bus fares. The church was a Church of
England, very cold and formal. I got lost
with which book I had to use and when to
use it! Needless to say, my attendance was
very patchy.

Entering my teenage years, my
relationship with Dad became very
stormy. We would have blazing rows,
usually ending with me storming out of
the house, shouting 'I'm leaving and
never coming back!', slamming the door
behind me. Relationships between my
parents were deteriorating also; there was
constant arguing and shouting.

The racist comments and name-calling followed me to the Senior School, but it was bearable because I had friends. School became my refuge.

Upon reaching third year we were sorted into groups according to ability. Amazingly, I was put in the top group. Linda B was in the second top group so we were separated during study time. I was in work class 301 and so was Gillian, who lived in my street! We became firm friends, walking to and from school together. As well as French, we now had the option to learn German as well. Walking home together from school we would practice our phrases or memorise the rhymes given:

'Dative preps are very few
Aus, Bei, mit, nach, zeit, von, zu!'

On one occasion walking home, we got talking about church. Gillian said she used to go to the Baptist Church in South Bank (where I'd attended Brownies) and wouldn't mind going back again. We made a plan to go that weekend.

Sunday came, Gillian called for me and we nervously made our way to church. We slipped into one of the pews. The hymns were meaningful, sung with great enthusiasm and gusto. Songs such as, "What a Friend we have in Jesus", "Great is Thy Faithfulness" and "Praise the Lord, Praise the Lord, Let the Earth Hear His Voice". We also sang choruses I had learnt at the Christian Union. A children's talk was given, then the Sunday School went out to their lessons. Gillian and I considered ourselves too old for Sunday School and stayed to hear the sermon delivered by the Pastor Dave. At the end of the service several people came to chat with us; everyone was very friendly and welcoming. On leaving, Pastor Dave was at the door, ready to shake our hands and encourage us to visit again. We needed no encouragement. Church became a regular occurrence, going to both morning and evening service.

I visited Gillian in her home; we went to the local youth club together. Her parents held a weekly disco, so I went along. We danced to 'Aviva Espania' and Showaddywaddy's 'Under the Moon of Love'. Gillian had learnt ballroom as a young child so learnt fairly quickly. I had two left feet and struggled to learn a simple routine.

Boys!!

"I've found a friend
oh such a friend,
who loved me
ere I knew Him"

Boys were strangers. Totally alien beings.
Loud and obnoxious, and who I mainly
ignored. However, in third year I became
aware of most of the girls talking more
and more about boys, who they liked and
who was going out with whom. I began to
think perhaps I should have a boyfriend or
at least show an interest in boys; I didn't
want to be left out. I looked around for a
suitable candidate. That boy who sat down
the left-hand side of the class looked
good: dark hair, dark eyes, attractive
smile, very handsome. He would do
nicely! It was only later I discovered I had
chosen Mark, top of the class! Not only
good-looking but intelligent, too. I set out
to discover all I could about Mark. I rarely
talked to the boys; the only interaction I
had was when they borrowed a pen or

ruler from me. Gillian, who had lots of male cousins, had no such inhibitions. She told me about Mark and kept me up to date about him. He had a very clever sister who went to the grammar school. Mark wasn't interested in girls, full stop. His recreation time revolved around football in winter and cricket in summer. During wet break times he and his mates would play table cricket, using a ruler for the bat and scrunched up paper for a ball. Mark became an increasing part of my thoughts and dreams. I fabricated all sorts stories about the two of us, always ending in the two of us marrying and riding off into the sunset! I was quiet, shy, and awkward at school, always wary and unsure how I'd be received, but I was desperate for Mark to take notice of me. He already knew I fancied him; word had got out and we were both teased. I made it my aim to do better in class, always trying to beat him in tests.

I continued to attend church regularly sat through many a sermon, learning I was a sinner, needing to be saved. To be saved I had to entrust my life to Jesus, say sorry for the things I had done wrong, sorry for doing what I wanted rather than what Jesus wanted. I had to live as Jesus wanted me to do. Jesus is the only God. He came to earth as a man not only to show us how to live but to die for our sins. Over time I realised I needed to ask Jesus to be my Lord and Saviour. He would forgive me so that I could belong to Him, even though I didn't deserve it. He would help me to live the life He had planned for me. It would be His righteousness, given to me as a gift if I would receive it. Jesus loved me enough to become a man for my sake and to die for my sins. Each Sunday evening Pastor Dave would invite those who wanted to entrust their lives to Jesus to walk out to the front of the church. I was too shy and scared. Several weeks passed when I did nothing. On one of our walks home from school Gillian confided that she too wanted to go out to the front. I said if she went I would go with her. Next Sunday we walked to the front! After the service those who had 'gone forward' were taken into one of the church's smaller rooms. Pastor Dave explained to us the need to turn from our current lives of doing want we wanted and to start living for Jesus Christ. He gave us each a prayer written on a scrap of paper. If we really wanted Jesus in our lives we were to go away, think things over, and say the prayer on our own to Jesus. I went home, and that night I knelt by my bed and said the prayer:

'Jesus, I have sinned, I have done wrong things, thought wrong things. I'm sorry. I want to turn away and live to please you. Amen.'

However, I added, 'If you really exist please show me, help me to get to know Mark more!'

Gillian told me she had also said the prayer. We told Pastor Dave. As so many young people had now shown an interest in Christ he decided to get the youth group up and running again. There was to be a meeting in the church hall after the evening service.

We sat around in a circle, Gillian and I next to each other. We went around the circle and took turns introducing ourselves. Gillian first, then myself, then the girl next to me spoke. She was very ' well spoken, had short, dark hair, and was good looking. She was older, and was about to go to university. Her name was Anne Adamson. "What's so special about that?" you may say. Anne Adamson was Mark's older sister! This wasn't her local church. What were the chances of that! This was my answer from God. Jesus existed! He heard and answered my silly prayer! The rest of the meeting was a blur. That night when I got home I knelt and prayed. I thanked God for answering me, for showing me He existed, and that I truly believed in Him. Jesus had come to live in me. He had taken away my sins. I knew He had made me a new person on the inside. I was one of God's children now, I had been born again.

Pastor Dave said I had to tell my parents what I had done. They did not fully understand; Dad asked if I was going to be a nun! I began to go to discipleship classes held at Dave's house. Sin was explained to us; murder, stealing, and lying to name but a few. I hadn't killed anyone, but I was guilty of many others. Dave explained using passing an exam as an example. If the pass mark was, say, 50%, one got 1% and another got 49%, both had failed! Because we are born in sinful flesh and blood we all have sinned; it's impossible for us to pass the exam.

"For ALL have sinned and come short of the glory of God." (Romans 3:20

God the Father is holy and cannot look on sin. Sin, therefore, separates us from God. The payment for sin is death. God does not want to be separated from us. He loves us. He loves us so much he decided to send His son Jesus Christ. Jesus was born without sin; He was both man and God. Jesus paid the price for my sin. He took my punishment so I don't have to pay it. He died on the cross, His sinless blood shed on my behalf. Jesus' death on the cross made a way (a bridge) between myself and God the Father. Now I can pray to Him anytime, knowing He will hear me.

"For the wages of sin is death, but the gift of God is eternal life through Jesus Christ our Lord." (Romans 16:24

I was thirsty for Jesus; I wanted to learn as much as possible. Once a week there was a prayer meeting before school, held at Dave's house. I gained such strength and comfort from that time.

Uncertain Times

*"If any man will come after me, let
him deny himself, and take up his
cross and follow me."*

Matt 16:24

Dad had been sacked! He had fought with
a fellow workman. Money became tighter
than ever. Tensions at home rose. Dad
was invited to help in my uncle's small
clothes shop. Uncle was going for a visit
back to India and wanted Mam and Dad to
run the shop while he was away.

Mam juggled serving customers and
looking after Beverley, now starting to
toddle around. Angela and I got a bus
from school and met them at the shop. We
all worked long hours, and all weekends.

For as long as I could remember, Dad was
'ordinary'. He mixed with both English
and Indian easily, eating whatever they
ate.

Strangely, Dad started to become 'more
Indian'. The statues of Indian gods
stopped being mere ornaments. Dad

started praying to them on a regular basis. Angela, who wanted to be all Indian and not English, copied him. He stopped eating beef and began to observe the Hindu festivals.

The shop wasn't doing very well, despite all our efforts. Customers liked Aunty Roma and did not welcome the change in staff. Takings went down, and, all in all, Dad (and Mam) became very stressed. Dad was so tired, he became very impatient with Mandy and Beverley; he did not tolerate noise. He began to punish Mandy and Beverley, and to a lesser extent Angela and me, by tapping us with a long thin bamboo cane. It got to the stage where he only had to pick it up and we were terrified. Dad had always been strict with us, not allowing us to swear, ensuring we dressed modestly, but I do not remember him hitting us until this time.

Dad was lying on the settee. He had a migraine and had taken strong pain killers. Mam sat on the chair besides the fire, her tea (in the North the evening meal is referred to as Tea) on her knee. Beverley began crying and trying to climb into her lap. Dad completely lost it. He jumped up off the settee, and tried to hit Beverley with his leather slipper. Mam sought to defend Beverley so Dad turned on her and hit her with his slipper, several hard slaps on her bare legs.

Next day returning from school, Mam informed me she had reported Dad to the police and they were coming to arrest him. I was sworn to secrecy. My emotions were in turmoil. I loved both Mam and Dad. Later that day Dad was arrested and held at the local police station. When released, he wasn't allowed to return to our home. Mam filed for divorce.

It took about a year for the divorce to come through. Dad lived in a flat above my uncle's shop. He accused me of taking Mam's side. Angela visited Dad regularly, sometimes taking Mandy and Beverley. I went as little as possible.

Stephens Road

"Do not worry about your life,
what you will eat or drink;...."
Matt 16:24-34

A condition of the divorce was the Warwick Street house had to be sold and the profits divided between Mam and Dad. About two weeks before my end of school exams and my 15th birthday, we moved to a council house in Stephens Road. There were three bedrooms. Angela declared she didn't like sleeping on her own and shared with Mandy. I had the little box room at the front of the house above the front door. Beverley shared the double bed with Mam.

I started taking Beverley and Mandy to Sunday School, to give Mam a break. Pastor Dave visited regularly to see if we were okay. Each Sunday upon leaving church, he would shake my hand and ask 'how are you?' I replied automatically, 'fine'. He would look at me as if to say, 'I know you're not!'

Jesus was my rock and my strength in those days. I clung to Him. He was the only one I could talk to.

Mam became reclusive, refusing to go outside the house. Angela or I took Beverley and Mandy to and from school, and did all the grocery shopping. Mam became ill. She couldn't get out of bed, couldn't eat. We didn't know what to do. Elaine a friend of mine visited, saw the situation, and went home and told her mum. Her mum came and talked to Mam, but she was too ill to understand. Mam was like this for about three or four days. The doctor had stopped prescribing Valium, a highly addictive anti-depressant. Mam had withdrawal symptoms. She went from weighing 13 stone to about six stone. Gradually she recovered and began to eat simple food. Angela and I did the house cleaning, cooking, and cared for Mandy and Beverley. We eventually got back to school regularly.

One day I came home to find Mam talking to two ladies. These ladies were dressed all in black and wore funny little hats. They were Ann and Glenda from the Salvation Army. Dave had heard of our situation and asked them to visit. Whilst chatting, Mam told them I was a Christian and went to church. Ann talked to Mam about Jesus. Handing me her telephone number she told me if I ever needed help I could call her day or night.

During this time Dad had gone back to India to visit his sisters and their families. We couldn't call on him for help. Dad wrote to us from India. Angela wanted an Indian husband and asked would he find one for her. I told her Jesus would find my husband. Someone called Tony, an acquaintance of Dad's, started to visit our house. He was very friendly. He brought a new-fangled video machine and we watched "Digby, the Biggest Dog in the World". He said he had a nice big house for us in the town centre and he would help us find Indian husbands. I told him I was a Christian and God would find me a husband. I was terrified Mam would accept his offer. I tried to think where I would live if she did, because I wouldn't be going! Unbeknownst to me Ann was praying about this, too. Thankfully nothing came of it, and Tony stopped visiting.

Coming of Age

"For I know the plans I have for you,"
declares the Lord,
"Plans to prosper you and not to harm
you,
Plans to give you a hope and a future"
Jeremiah 29:11

I passed my end of school exams. I
wanted to be a nurse but had to wait until I
was 18 to start training. Although I didn't
need further qualifications, I decided to go
to Sixth Form College until I was old
enough; besides, Mark was going! Sixth
Form was very different; no uniform for a
start, and lessons were less formal. My
friends began meeting for drinks in pubs,
girls began whispering in groups about
their new experiences with their
boyfriends. I had no interest in these
things and felt left out. My social life
consisted of going to youth fellowship.
Occasionally we drove out to the North
Yorkshire Moors and played wide games
(a little like hide & seek) or just enjoyed
the walks. We ended the day by going to

little country inns and sharing a meal together. I went on annual hikes with the church and attended the Easter Sunrise service. Walking a mile to the foot of Cleveland Hills at about 5 am and then walking up a hill to watch the sunrise, we would sing and praise the Lord, for He had conquered death and risen from the grave. These were much more meaningful than going to a noisy pub, full of smoke, where you couldn't hear each other.

Sixth Form held regular discos and I was allowed to go to one. Mam agreed I could go, so long as I walked back in a group with Gillian and others. She gave me the back door key to get in, as we didn't have a spare front door one.

We had a great night! Obediently, I walked home with Gillian and friends, laughing and joking. We parted company to go to our separate homes—Gillian to Warwick Street and me to Stephens Road. I got the key ready and made my way to the back of the house. Hmm, strange, there was a light glowing just round the corner. Had Mam left the kitchen light on? Going closer, I could see the light was coming from the shed, the door open. I heard Mam call, 'Linda, help me'. As my eyes focused quickly taking in the scene. I saw Mam standing on something, clutching something hanging from the ceiling. She was attempting to hang herself! Somehow Mam was persuaded down and I got her back into the house. Running upstairs, I woke up Angela. She sat with Mam whilst I went in search of a phone box. On the way I bumped into Ross (Julie's uncle), a family friend. He let me use his friend's house phone. I phoned Ann and told her what'd happened. Ross obviously heard the conversation and insisted on coming back with me. Ann was coming but she lived a half-hour car journey away. Ross went to investigate the shed. I sat numb. Ann came and talked to Mam and made sure she was safe. Turning to me she asked, "What about you, are you okay?" I insisted I was, but both she and I knew I wasn't! I don't know if I slept that night, it's all a blur now. I do remember going back to college and being unable to focus or concentrate on anything. I kept replaying the shed scene in my mind. I couldn't share with my friends. They wouldn't understand; they had normal families where they laughed and had fun. I couldn't laugh. I spent my free time sitting around the college corridors, staring out the windows. My work suffered. I missed a lot of college. Mam needed constant watching. Other attempts were made. We woke in the middle of the night to find her with a knife in her hand! Sometimes she'd take an overdose and spend a night in hospital. Each time Ann was true to her word and came out day or night. Ann and Glenda took turns in taking Mandy and Beverley to stay with them, but I still got so far behind with my studies it was impossible to catch up. I re-assured myself it was okay because I'd been accepted for nursing.

Mam had been attending the Baptist Church for some time. Looking after four children purely on state benefits was a constant struggle. We often ran out of food at the end of the week. Mam would go without so we could eat. Sometimes we would open our front door to find a food parcel on the step, or simply a bunch of flowers. They always arrived just when we most needed them. One Christmas Mam had no gifts for us. The church heard, and one by one people brought dolls, a buggy, dolls clothes, teddy bears. Mandy and Beverley had their 'Merry Little Christmas'. Angela and I weren't forgotten; we were given small gifts from Social Services and the Salvation Army.

Eventually Mam gave her life to Jesus. There was a gradual change, but the most dramatic was when she stopped smoking 60 cigarettes a day. She expressed a desire to give up but struggled to do so. I and another church member prayed with her. Virtually overnight she stopped smoking. The Lord began piecing her life back together. She went to the weekly coffee morning and enjoyed washing the dishes and talking with the ladies.

Meanwhile, I continued to struggle with my studies. Finals were looming. I spent hours trying to revise all the notes I had. The information just wouldn't stay, and there were huge gaps in my notes. I went to the three-hour exams, knowing I couldn't write for that long. Sixth Form came to an end. I had been accepted for nurse training subject to passing a medical.

I had decided to make the most of this summer. It was June, my birthday month. A few days before, Mam took another overdose. Angela was working away from home and I was alone. Again, Ann came. Mam was taken and kept in hospital. I took care of myself, Beverley, and Mandy over the next few days, but without Angela I couldn't cope. I phoned Ann in tears. Ann again drove down. This time she took the three of us to her house, to stay with her, her husband, and two children. We slept in Ann's front room on an air bed. Next morning Ann came in with a small present for me. It was the morning of my 18th birthday!

Fellowship And Love

"A new commandment I give you
Love one another.....
By this everyone will know that you are
my disciples"
John 13:34-35

True to his word, Dave arranged an
interview for a position at a place called
Brockley Hall to become part of the
domestic staff. It was in Saltburn by the
Sea, too far to travel daily. I would have
to live in, returning home on my days off.
The interview was a mere formality, I was
offered the job with a year's contract.

On my arrival I was shown to an attic
room, containing two single beds. I was
told one belonged to a girl called Mandy,
who I'd be sharing with.

Brockley Hall was owned by the
Methodist Association. It was a Christian
Guest House, offering holiday
accommodation to various Christian
groups. My day started at am. My first

duties were to dust, polish, and hoover the downstairs reception rooms. We then had staff breakfast. There was porridge, and several different cereals to choose from. Following this came a cooked breakfast of bacon and eggs (or whatever the guests were having that day). As if that wasn't enough, we then had toast and marmalade, all washed down with as much tea as you wanted. Once finished, it was all systems go to serve the guests breakfast. I carried large trays holding six bowls of porridge to each table. With breakfast over, we cleaned up the dining room and set the tables for lunch. After lunch I was allowed a couple of hours off-duty, which I used to explore the town of Saltburn. At pm I was back on duty, ready to serve dinner.

After dinner, guests were entertained in the drawing room. One night there would be a quiz, the next a games night, with carpet bowls competitions. We had dancing to the birdie song or the hokey cokey. Other nights there'd be a sing song, where we sang on Ilkley Mor by Tat, or Cockles and Mussels. The last night was always Concert Night.

Individuals from the holiday group would sign up to do their party pieces; it varied from recitals, to poems they'd written, or a beautiful solo of 'Drink to me Only with Thine Eyes'. Every evening ended with an Epilogue. Someone would read a scripture, share a little about it, and then say a prayer.

Cocoa and biscuits or a piece of cake had to be served before I could finally fall into bed. The alarm rang at am and it all started again!

With good food, and hard work in a friendly, loving environment, I blossomed. I grew in confidence and was, on the whole, cheerful. I laughed and joked with staff and guests alike.

On Sundays I was allowed to attend a church of my choice in the evening (mornings were busy with guests). I went to The Mission, a small Brethren Church across the road from Brockley Hall. Occasionally Mandy came too, and Robin, the junior chef. They took me to the home of Terry and Margaret, their friends.

Terry and Margaret had a teenage daughter and opened their house to young people working at Brockley or who attended the Mission. We could drop in any time we were off-duty for a coffee and chat.

A Teens and Twenties group started to meet in their home on Tuesday evenings. In the winter season when Brockley was less busy, we were allowed time off to attend. We shared things that troubled us, prayed for one another, and were taught the scriptures by Ron, an elder in the church. This 'Teens & Twenties' Group consisted of members whose ages ranged from 16 to about 50+ years. There was Marion and Joan, two older ladies who I worked with at Brockley, and Big Dave, a man in his late twenties who was a very new Christian, to name but a few. We began a study on the Ten Commandments. Ron was an excellent teacher and gave us a good understanding of Bible history, and the best explanation of each commandment I have ever had to this day! We grew very close as a group and went on a study weekend to Whitby. It was such a precious time.

Back at home, Mam supported by the Baptist Church, grew from strength to strength. Angela had become a Christian. Ann taught us all about the dangers of worshipping other gods, the demonic power we were exposing ourselves to. She told how reading and following horoscopes was of the devil. Hindu religion is steeped in superstition; many marriages are arranged according to horoscope signs. Once Angela gave her life to the Lord Jesus, we emptied our home of any statues or pictures of Hindu deities. Horoscope books were burnt.

At Brockley I had my own quiet time with the Lord. In the summer I would walk to a small secluded waterfall, sit on a log, and pray. I poured my heart out to Jesus, gave all my concerns to Him. In winter I'd shut myself away in one of the empty bedrooms of Brockley.

After I had been at Brockley for six months I began to ask the Lord what he wanted me to do next; after all, I was only here for a year. The call to be a missionary was still there. Talking to others I was told I would need to go to bible college. Ron gave me the names of a few to apply to. I was accepted at Lebanon Missionary Bible College (LMBC) at Berwick-upon-Tweed.

In September 1982, I travelled to LMBC and Angela moved into Brockley Hall to take my place. Brockley Hall had been a good preparation for Bible College. My day began very similarly. Wake up am, then Quiet Time. To keep the costs down, every student was expected to do daily duties, whether it be cleaning, serving or preparing food, washing up, etc., all carried out on a rota system. Most cleaning duties were performed in the morning before breakfast. After breakfast came assembly and then the day's lessons until pm, with an hour's break for lunch. Evening study time was from 6:30 until pm.

Lessons were not restricted to the classrooms. LMBC had students from many denominations and many countries. Adapting to each other's ways did not always go smoothly. There was the time two room-mates argued over whose turn it was to empty the bin; the argument continued so long that eventually it was impossible to see the bin for rubbish! Or the unfortunate one who had to share with a room-mate who snored. In my second year I was in a four-bed room at the very top of the house. One lady (Rachel) was from Manchester and the other two were from Germany. We learnt much from each other. The German girls, (Hannah & Elise) although they lived in Germany, had originally come from Russia. Hearing their stories about the dangers of practising their faith was inspiring. They filled our room with music and song. They made the most of every opportunity, during exam time often studying (in a third language) into the early hours of the morning. Denise, the lady from Manchester, loved to re-arrange the furniture in our room. We'd come back from lessons, go to make a cup of coffee at the little table where we kept our kettle, only the table wasn't there! It had been moved to a different corner. Or someone may have left a blouse or jumper on their bed, only for it to disappear to an unknown drawer. I found it amusing, but the German girls didn't! On the other hand, the German girls would walk into the room and immediately open the window wide, even on a cold winter's day. Denise and I didn't like this! Tensions rose until it got to a point where we had to sit down and talk. Denise agreed not to move personal belongings and the German girls agreed to ask before opening the window.

Operation Mobilisation

"Therefore go and make disciples of all nations,
Baptizing them in the name of the Father and of the Son and of the Holy Spirit, teaching them to obey everything I have commanded you"
Matt:28:19-20

In the summer of my first year, I spent a month working with Operation Mobilisation, an organisation where young Christians could learn how to share the Gospel with others. They taught young people around the world to preach in the Streets, to go from door to door selling bibles and Christian books, and to help local churches evangelise their own countries. There was a week's convention held in Leuven, Belgium which all summer campaigners had to attend. On Friday 29th July 1983, I left home at about am. The coach journey to London took five hours. Arriving in Victoria Bus Station I sat down and attempted to eat something, but I had developed a migraine during the journey so could only manage to drink a little and eat an apple. I then set about finding the correct train to Herne Hill. Eventually I arrived at the right platform and met up with Karen (from LMBC) and some of her friends from Northern Ireland. It was so much better travelling as a group. We arrived at Herne Hill Baptist Church at pm, where we were given our ferry tickets and a cup of tea. By this time, I was feeling really ill and had to make a dash for the toilets. I thought I would never make it across the Channel; we hadn't even started the sea journey and I was getting seasick! At pm, we left the church for the ferry port of Folkestone. At last, I was starting to feel a little better. We made it to Folkestone by 1080p, and had another hour to wait for the ferry. Many were pretty tired by this time, but some people started playing guitars and singing choruses. I discovered we could praise God even though we were tired. The ferry arrived an hour later than scheduled, so we boarded at am on Saturday. Going through Customs seemed to take forever. Once aboard we saw all seats were taken and so found a space on the floor near to the toilets. I had started to feel ill again. I must have dozed off for a few minutes, for I was woken by a girl offering me her seat. I took up the offer and made myself comfortable. I slept the rest of the night, waking at am. This was my first time outside of the United Kingdom and it was strange to see the sea outside the window. Shortly, announcements were made in French, German, and English that we were nearing land.

Once in Belgium we made our way through Customs and on to the railway station. Two hundred young people from England boarded the train for Leuven. From Leuven we were taken by bus to the college where our conference was to be held. It was a sprawling stone-built structure set in extensive grounds. Along one verandah was a long line of tables. Here we filled in various forms, then we joined what seemed like another endless queue in order to get our room number. I was given the same room as Karen and her companions from Northern Ireland, plus one other girl. The room was on the second floor at the end of a long dark corridor. The room itself was very basic: there were six army-style beds, five along one wall and one under a window at the end. Quickly we unpacked our sleeping bags, then went in search of the showers. We found them in the cellars; at first sight they made me think of a row of prison cells. The refreshing hot shower soon dispelled such thoughts. It was now lunchtime so we made our way to the dining room. After eating nothing but snacks and sandwiches for two days I was looking forward to a substantial meal. My heart sank when I saw the dark green liquid in my bowl. Spinach soup! I had never been keen on soup. Grace was said and I tentatively tasted the soup; it wasn't as bad as it looked. From that moment I decided I would not make a fuss about the food, but eat whatever I was given. The meal finished I made my way to bed, wondering just what I had let myself in for.

Operation Mobilisation focused on sharing the Good News with people through literature written in their own language. I was to be part of a team reaching out to Asians in Britain. Part of our training involved depending upon God for our daily needs, our food, toiletries, petrol, etc. We spent this week in Leuven, searching the scriptures, worshipping the Lord Jesus, and praying for the summer work.

930 young people from many nations worshipping together is a powerful thing to witness.

During the five days that followed we were divided into groups of fifty then smaller groups of ten. Each group of ten was assigned daily duties to perform. Our group's duty was to clean the kitchens. The first time I was allotted the ovens to clean. Next time around I volunteered to go down into the basement, as I thought it would be easier, but how wrong I was! Grease had spilt all over the floor, we were sliding all over, it was like an ice rink. Taking a deep breath, I rolled up my sleeves and set to work with buckets of hot water and cloths. Just as soon as I got a section clean, the drain would overflow and so I had to begin all over again! Eventually water and grease would not stop coming up out of the drain, so one of the men came to help. We had to carry away buckets of food slops which had blocked the drain. Once this had been done, the floor could be cleaned at last. Again and again, the man came back scooping all the smelly food slops up into the large industrial dustbins. Some of the other girls helped him. I said to myself, 'I'm not doing that!' I knew this was the wrong attitude, yet still I didn't help.

It was am. I was packing my things as quietly as possible. Yesterday I had said my farewells to those staying in mainland Europe, for today I would travel to Greenwich, London where I put into practice all I had learnt.

My home for the next three weeks was a sprawling Baptist Church in Greenwich. The men camped in the larger church hall, whilst the girls set out their sleeping bags in one of the side rooms. We had to pack away our belongings whenever the rooms were used for church meetings. We had the kitchen at our disposal and a large room which served as both dining room and meeting room. We depended upon the hospitality of church members for showers. Our mornings were spent in group devotions. We were a team of eleven: Savi, Benita, Christina, Irene, Margarita, Christina II, and I made up the girls. Jeff (team leader), Lars, Adrian, and Martin made up the boys. We were expecting a married couple, Chuck and Sue, to join us in a few days. All were assigned daily duties. I was placed in charge of cooking until Sue and Chuck arrived.

Our afternoons and evenings were spent going to different areas in Greenwich, knocking on doors, hoping to share the Gospel and give out literature. Due to my cooking duties my afternoons were cut short, as I needed to return to the church earlier to prepare the meals. As well as preparing the meals, all ingredients had to be purchased. We had no income, so we asked God for everything. This meant being very imaginative when creating meals. More and more meal planning dominated my thoughts, making it difficult to concentrate during prayer meetings. At one meeting I asked the Lord to provide a frying pan. Later that day a member of the church called; they had baked scones for us and also thought we might 'find a use' for their spare frying pan!

On our last evening Jeff told us we did not have enough petrol to get us back to Central London, where we would all go our separate ways. One of the girls shared how the Lord provides exactly what we need at exactly the right time. He is never too early or too late. She had just finished sharing when one of the church deacons came and gave us a gift of £10. This was the exact amount needed to get us all back home. Many had tears in their eyes. God had proved so faithful throughout our time together.

At the end of my second year of Bible college, Operation Mobilisation gave permission for myself and a girl called Jacqui to join their India Mission. It was unusual because we were going for three months, and normally they did not accept anyone for less than two years. God faithfully provided the finances so that I could go. We were due to fly at the end of June. There was just one small problem. My visa had not arrived! I phoned the Indian Embassy and they said I may collect it from the Embassy in person, but there was no guarantee it would be ready. We flew on the 27th. I had to collect the visa on the 25th (my 21st birthday). A few days before starting out on the journey to London, Angela told me there was to be a farewell meeting for me at church. Walking into the church hall I was greeted by very dear friends and family. I soon realised this was not only a farewell meeting but also a 21st birthday party for me, the one and only birthday party I'd ever had! Angela had made the cake, beautifully decorated with a picture of the Taj Mahal. Early on the 25th I made the four-hour train journey to London and made my way to the Embassy. It was a hot day and the queue seemed to go on forever. I took my place, took out my bible, and prayed desperately for this visa.

My flight was booked, everything arranged, Jacqui was waiting for me at her house in London, but without the visa I could go nowhere. Eventually I reached the desk and explained my dilemma to the clerk. He looked around the office and said, 'I can't see it. Let me just go ask my colleagues.' After a bit of rummaging at the back of the office he waved my visa in the air, 'Praise the Lord!' I shouted. Jesus had worked yet another miracle.

After a 14-hour flight our plane started to descend into Bombay Airport. On its descent all I could see was row upon row of corrugated roof tops, home to the poor of India.

We spent a few days at Operation Mobilisation (OM) Headquarters before starting a train journey that took us right across from West to East India. We travelled in a ladies only compartment, apparently less crowded than the rest of the train. The train had a huge great black steam engine, like something from Edwardian times. The journey took two days and one night. During that time a couple of Mother Theresa's nuns shared our compartment. Whenever the train stopped at a station our window was bombarded with a constant stream of beggars or hawkers selling food. The nuns always handed out food to the beggars.

The train took us to Calcutta where we borded a smaller train to our destination in Orissa. We were surprised at how easily we found two seats in a fairly quiet part of the train. When we disembarked we found the reason why! The benches had been newly painted and I had the dark red marks on my light blue Salwar (trousers) to prove it!

Part of my time in India was spent with the West Bengal OM (Operation Mobilisation) Team. This was so I could go visit my relatives. Jacqui stayed in Orissa. It meant I was the only English person on the team. I looked Indian, but I wasn't totally and I didn't speak the language. It was a time of much soul searching. I wasn't Indian and I wasn't English; where did I fit in? I wanted a husband, did God want that for me? I spent much time alone, asking God for His direction. I eventually found peace, bowing my will to that of the Lord. If Jesus wanted me single for the rest of my life, so be it. He would give me the strength for this. I would be obedient and serve Him on the mission field. The questions followed me back to England and back to Bible College. I was restless, depressed, and unable to concentrate. My tutor arranged counselling sessions for me.

My third and final year. I was going to concentrate on my studies and go back to India. That year Angela had decided to come to LMBC also. I had the opportunity of living outside of the college, in the town of Berwick itself. I shared a room with Liz in a place called Fields House. As a result, I wasn't at college when all the residential students arrived, and it was a few days before I saw Angela. I had however read the list of names pinned to the notice board in the common room. Standing in my favourite spot, near the radiator in front of the big window, I noticed a new student sitting in the armchair there. I was introduced to Angus (Gus) Graham; a good Scottish name! I listened to him chatting away to Angela and thought, that's not a Scottish accent. I said as much to him and asked where he was from. 'Durham' came the reply. Oh good, someone who lived fairly near me! We chatted on and it turned out he had his own car and had driven here (a rarity at LMBC). 'Oh good, I responded. "Can I have a lift home?"

From then on, we often bumped into each other and occasionally Gus would give me a lift back to Fields House. One evening before getting out of the car, I said, 'Angela tells me there's gossip about you and me. People are wondering what's going on, whether we are going out together'. I said, 'As far as I'm concerned, I'm in third year and you're in first, at the end of the year I'm going on the mission field, so as far as I'm concerned I'm not interested in any relationship'. On that note, I said good night and got out of the car.

Graduation

*"So do not fear, for I am with you;
do not be dismayed, for I am your God.
I will strengthen you and help you;
I will uphold you with my righteous right
hand"*

Isaiah 41:10

'Ouch, that hurt!'. Hannah was arranging my hair into a plaited crown adorned with fresh laburnum flowers. The whole of the girl's sleeping quarters was filled with a hustle & bustle as we dressed in our best outfits. It was graduation day! I wore a dark green silk sari covered in gold embroidery. It belonged to Mam, who had gifted it to me for the occasion. A couple of church members had offered to drive Mam up to college for the ceremony. The afternoon was filled with voices praising God for His goodness during our time at LMBC. Speeches were made and we were presented with our certificates. A flurry of photographs were taken, refreshments served. I was full of mixed emotions. Proud to have graduated, but also sad. After spending three years together, praying, learning, supporting and growing together. Now we were parting, scattering to different parts of the world. Many I would never see again.

Gus and I had continued our friendship during the last year. Driving to Bamburgh Castle and walking along the beach, confiding and helping one another through difficult times. Yet, we couldn't commit to any formal relationship. We longed to hold hands, kiss, but we were going to different parts of the world. It wasn't sensible to take things any further than friendship. As Gus' home was only an hour away from mine, I knew I would see him again after today, but it would be less often. Not on a daily basis as it had been for the past year.

"Would you like to come out for a meal with me tonight? ", Gus whispered, whilst posing for one of the many photos taken that day. We waved goodbye to the last of the guests. I quickly changed out of my Sari into something more practical but I left the flowers in my hair. Gus looked very smart in his suit. We drove into Berwick-upon-Tweed, parked in the market place and made our way to the small hotel. It was extremely busy and we had to wait for a table. The hotel was filled with LMBC students. It wasn't long before some friends spotted us and invited us to join their group. Several couples were already seated when we reached the table. We had an enjoyable evening, but Gus and I longed for some time alone. After the meal we separated from the rest of the group and went for a walk along the beach.

Upon finishing Bible College in the summer of 1985, I returned home to Stephens Road. I had been asked to spend time in my home church before being considered for overseas work. I taught in Sunday School, assisted at Boys and Girls Club, and spoke at the Ladies Meeting. I thoroughly enjoyed teaching Sunday School. I taught the youngest class, 2-3 year olds. The children that came to the Sunday School came from very deprived families. On one occasion, a child came in thin clothes and bare feet; it was the middle of winter with frost on the ground!

The following summer a team from OM came to our church and we began reaching out to the Asian community in our area. We knocked on doors and shared the Good News of Christ's love for them. We always went in twos. I was paired with Joyce, another Sunday School teacher. On some occasions we had some rather unsavoury invitations from Asian men. We had more success talking to the Asian women, many of whom I had known from childhood. At the end of the two-week campaign we had a film evening, with specially prepared Indian food for refreshments. Many of the Asian ladies and their children attended. After the OM team had left, Joyce and I continued to visit these families. Once Angela finished Bible college she continued the ministry, helping those who had suffered domestic abuse.

I enrolled on a typing and shorthand course, went to keep fit classes, basically I kept myself busy. Throughout this time

Gus and I wrote to each other. As my plans to go to India had come to a halt, I sought the Lord as to the next step. Gus invited me along to a weekend missionary conference. The Society hosting it, worked primarily in East Africa.

December 16th 1986, Gus proposed. The pastor had given us permission to use a room at church for our Bible study and prayer, as there were no spare rooms or quiet spaces at my home. That evening, before the cross in the main meeting room, Gus going down on both knees asked me to marry him. Of course, I said yes! We both knelt before the Lord and committed ourselves to Him. We decided to get engaged on Christmas Eve. A few days beforehand we got up at an extremely early hour and took the train to Preston in Lancashire. A friend had purchased their ring from this particular jeweller and I wanted to look there first for my ring. The jewellers really made it a special occasion. We were given our own private seating area and served coffee and chocolates. The ring chosen, a small diamond surrounded by six sapphires, it was placed in a green velvet box in the shape of a book. We had a photo taken which fitted in the lid of the box. When opened it revealed not only the photo but also a personal message embossed in gold lettering.

I clutched that little jeweller's bag very carefully, grinning like a Cheshire Cat all the way home. Once back at Stephens Road, we settled down to watch TV with the rest of the family. As the evening wore on the rest of the family gradually made their way to bed. Gus was staying at ours. I had given up my room and was to sleep in a sleeping bag on the floor of Angela and Mandy's room. Alone at last, I began to sense something was wrong Eventually, with tears streaming down his face, Gus said he was having doubts about getting married. I thought it was just nerves, but then I got scared. Gus was crying and rolling about in agony. I told Gus if he was unsure and wanted to call the engagement off then he must say so. I said this, not thinking it would really happen, but it DID! I was completely stunned, numb. I couldn't believe this was happening. We agreed Gus would leave early next morning. All we could do was pray together before going to bed. Climbing into my sleeping bag, I cried the whole night through.

Next morning, I was up before Gus. Everyone thought I was excited and kept going on about the ring. Eventually Gus came downstairs, refusing offers of breakfast, then he went into the kitchen and tearfully explained to Mam. We then broke the news to my sisters. It was so hard. I dreaded Christmas Day; my best Christmas had turned into the worst! How I got through the next few days I don't know.

Gus talked things over with his own parents, we met with my minister, chatted, and prayed. The result of all these discussions was we agreed on a three-month separation to seek God's will. We agreed we wouldn't see, write, or contact each other during this time. The waiting was absolute agony; I was in limbo, not knowing what to do. I threw myself into work at church and kept myself as busy as possible. The Lord gave me a scripture which I clung to.

> *"Who shall separate us from the love of Christ? Shall trouble or hardship or persecution or famine or nakedness or danger or sword?*
>
> *As it is written:*
>
> *'For your sake we face death all day long;*
> *we are considered as sheep to be slaughtered.*
>
> *No, in all these things we are more than conquerors through him who loved us .[38] For I am convinced that neither death nor life, neither angels nor demons, neither the present nor the future, nor any powers, [39] neither height nor depth, nor anything else in all creation, will be able to separate us from the love of God that is in Christ Jesus our Lord.*
>
> *Romans 8:35-39*

I believed Jesus was saying "don't worry, everything will turn out fine" but it was difficult not to doubt.

On April 4th 1987, we got engaged. We both were absolutely certain this was God's will for us.

The Married Years

"Where you go I will go, and where you stay I will stay. Your people will be my people and your God my God"
Ruth 1:16

We married a year later on a sunny, but breezy, day in July, our reception being held at Brockley Hall.

We made our first home in a three-bedroom detached house in the suburbs of Durham near to Gus' parents and our work. Almost all our furniture had been donated by friends and family, with the exception of one or two brand new items which were wedding presents. In our living room we had two armchairs and a borrowed coffee table, nothing else!

We worked 9-5 each weekday. Our evenings and weekends were spent teaching the teenage Sunday school, preaching (Gus) or leading missionary meetings. We had applied and been accepted by a missionary organisation that worked in East Africa. Our task now was to share about the work in Africa, in particular Tanzania, where we hoped to go. The summer before we married, we had spent six weeks in Nigeria to get a taste of African culture.

Two years after our marriage I gave up my office job to care for our first child, Ruth. As well as caring for Ruth, I composed and typed our monthly newsletter, arranged and led coffee mornings in aid of our African Mission. We still led missionary meetings and we began introducing our 'African Nights'. We dressed in traditional African outfits (obtained in Nigeria) and cooked African food: rice, beans, and hot chilli sauce with chin chin, an African donut for dessert. Our Nigerian friends from Bible college helped. We showed slides, shared prayer requests, and shared our calling to go.

When Ruth was about ten months old, we were visited by a missionary couple from our mission society. They stayed a few days with us, assessing if we were suitable for the mission field, giving us help and advice on how to prepare.

We gave up our bedroom and slept in the spare room. I had the single bed and Gus slept on a Z-bed next to me. In order to get to Ruth during the night I had to climb over Gus' bed, so Gus offered to get Ruth and bring her to me for feeding.

During the day Angus was at the office, so I was left to entertain the missionary couple. I spent a lot of my time playing with Ruth.

Before our visitors left, the four of us sat around our dining table to discuss what had been observed. Gus was giving 70% effort and I only 30%. Gus was praised for the production of our monthly newsletter, the first he had written, as I was still adjusting to being a first-time mum. I had recovered slowly from the birth. He was praised for the African-themed nights (my idea).

I should be the one getting up to see to Ruth during the night, not Gus. It was suggested instead of making a Sunday roast to make something easier that could just be left in the oven. When at church Ruth could be left in the care of others whilst I participated more, and lastly, Ruth could be left to 'listen at the door' whilst I took part in the prayer meeting. Gus and I were stunned, speechless! I felt I had let him down; I was not good enough.

Despite the disastrous visit, we were accepted to work in Tanzania; enough funds had been raised and our visa granted. Then came a period of unrest in Tanzania and our departure was delayed. A condition of the Mission Society was that all missionaries had to have the approval of their home church. Up until this point we had the full support of the church leaders.

Two years after being accepted to go to Tanzania and following the birth of our second child, Beth, our church services changed. A different gospel was taught. Families received visits from the elders and were asked to accept this new way. Our turn came. We were visited by three of the four elders. We were told unless we accepted this new way, they would not support our mission application, and they would not send us overseas. The following Sunday, the elders stood at the front of the church and stated that all had to sign a contract agreeing to the new church regime. Those who refused to sign were asked to leave the church. As the new regime was not in accordance with what the Bible, the Word of God, taught, we had no option but to leave.

We eventually settled in a new church, which had a good Sunday School which taught the scriptures. Subsequently the Mission Society indicated, that because we had changed churches, we needed to spend time getting to know each other, and so our departure was yet again delayed. We needed the new church to agree to send us.

We were again visited and inspected by the elders of our new church. We were told they only ever sent the best! I was left wondering what was meant by best. Was it what they thought was best or what God saw as best! We never heard anything again. Our application to the Mission Society lapsed and we never got to Tanzania.

The Long Dark Tunnel

*My dove in the clefts of the rock,
In the hiding-places on the
mountainside, Show me your face,
Let me hear your voice; For your
voice is sweet, And your face is
lovely*
Song of Songs 2:14ff

In November 1996, Ruth was five years
old, Beth was three, and I was nine
months pregnant with our third child. My
father suffered a series of strokes and
subsequently died. During his visit to
India all those years ago, Dad had
remarried and had two sons. He was in the
process of divorcing his second wife at the
time of his death. Angela and I were the
executors of his will and, as such, had the
responsibility of emptying his house and
sorting his belongings. Except it wasn't
straight forward. His estranged wife
contested the will. Months and years of
legal wrangling followed, but in those first

weeks after Dad's death life was frantic, with much travelling to and fro.

Our third child, Aaron, was born in January. Life became a whirlwind of school drop-offs and pick-ups. I didn't seem to recover from this birth as I had with the previous two. After the birth of our daughters I had been able to return to the gym within a few months, this time it must have been about a year before I was able to go back. However, I couldn't get past the warm up before feeling extremely ill, to the point where I was going to throw up. I put it down to having three children and the extra work involved.

June 1997, it was my birthday. Gus and I were preparing for our first 'date' since Aaron's arrival. To celebrate, Gus bought tickets to see a West End production of 'Grease', which was touring the North-east. Just before we left for the theatre, the phone rang. It was Mam, calling I thought to wish Happy Birthday, which she did, but she was also very upset. She told me Angela was in hospital with a fractured jaw, a cut very near her eye, and other bruising, all inflicted in front of her three-year-old daughter.

By the time Aaron was two years old, my tiredness had not improved but had gotten steadily worse. Housework went undone. I snapped at the children; I couldn't bear noise. I was tearful and depressed. I would sleep twelve hours a night, yet wake up exhausted. We were about to go on our annual holiday. I had slept soundly the night before; we were all packed and on the road by am. Five minutes down the road and I was fast asleep again and stayed that way for the entire four-hour journey! Gus began to suspect something was wrong; we both did. After visits to the doctor, and various tests, which all came back negative, we were no further forward. Ann said it may be Myalgic Encephalomyelitis /Chronic Fatigue Syndrome, but my GP was adamant there was no such thing. Eventually in despair I saw a private doctor, who confirmed I had ME/CFS. I was given a protocol of vitamin supplements and told to rest. I went from being a fairly active mum, going to the gym three times a week, attending various groups with the children, and leading a house group with Gus, to being unable to perform normal household tasks without being exhausted. During the week I would struggle to care for the children's needs until Gus got home from work and took over. I took the children to school in the car (if I managed to get up at all; on those occasions Gus took them before going to work), then I'd rest until it was time for them to come home. I struggled on until Gus got in from work. He would get home to find nothing had been done, no hoovering, laundry, ironing. I couldn't stand noise and sometimes bright lights. As soon as Gus got home, I went upstairs to our room and stayed there till the next morning. I used the weekends to catch up on rest and recharge for the coming week. I stopped going to church; there was no energy for that, and the music was far too loud for me. I would find myself wanting to nod off during the service because I was so tired (not because of the speaker). I couldn't think straight, couldn't get my thoughts together to form prayers, couldn't concentrate to read my bible. I virtually cut myself off from everyone. I missed so much of our family life. Angus and the children would go on days out and I would have to stay behind because it was too tiring for me to walk or if it was the cinema because the noise was too loud.

Three years after my diagnosis the elderly doctor who had been treating me died and I had to find someone else who was well acquainted with ME. Through a fellow sufferer, I heard of a doctor in Bolton (2-3 hours away). I had to give a blood smear, which was then examined under an electron microscope. My blood was infected with bacteria called borellia, which causes the illness called Lyme Disease. It turned out I had Chronic Lyme Disease and not ME. These bacteria penetrate every part of the body; it gets into the neurological system and the brain. I was so relieved to find that I had not been imagining it all and that it wasn't just 'all in my head', but an actual physical illness. I was put on a strong course of antibiotics together with various vitamin supplements.

Over a period of two to three years there began to be some improvement in my condition. People had commented on my lack of church attendance or involvement and expressed concern about my spiritual condition. I have had great battles within myself and with the Lord about this. I felt so guilty not being able to do anything. Even reading my bible or praying was difficult, as I just could not concentrate or get my thoughts together especially when I had what is called brain fog. I felt unless I could contribute something to the church then people did not want to know. Most of my fellowship and encouragement came via the internet and Ann. I arranged to get daily readings sent to my email. Although I did not pray, or have a quiet time in the conventional sense, I talked to the Lord on and off throughout the day (and the night when I could not sleep) as I would a friend. God showed me that even before I knew Him He loved me. Before I was involved with church, Sunday school, or any other type of service, He loved me. He knew I was ill and He loved me whether I could serve Him or not. I didn't have to do anything for Jesus to love me.

No matter what my fellow Christians thought of me, no matter how I was judged on how little I could do, I *know* Jesus loves me. He remained faithful. In one of my daily readings the writer described how on their drive to work they would pass mountains and on some mornings those mountains would be invisible to them because of the morning mist. They explained that sometimes though it feels as though our prayers are not getting through and we can't feel God's presence with us, God is still with us through the mist. This illustration has stayed with me through the years and has been a great comfort.

In May 2004, Gus was taken into hospital with breathing problems. They decided to keep him in for a week to do tests. I was suddenly left alone to cope with looking after the children and the house, plus being worried about Gus. I phoned the church care/prayer team to let them know and for them to pray. I also asked for practical help perhaps with meals, as it was difficult to fit in making them in between visiting. I was on the phone every day to Ann, in floods of tears, panicking as to how I was going to cope. Rushing in and out to hospital and walking up the long hospital corridors twice a day, plus the stress of worrying about Gus (also having to deal with cancelling our holiday) was exhausting enough. At one visiting time a member of the care team came to visit Gus and prayed with us. I got the impression of it being a case of 'see you can do it if you really try and pull yourself together'. When Gus came home from hospital (having been given a clean bill of health), I felt guilty because I practically fell into bed exhausted. It took weeks, perhaps months, before Gus or I got back to some resemblance of normality.

At the end of September 2004, Angela was taken into hospital. She had gone into work that morning (Wednesday), complained of her head hurting, and collapsed. Arriving at the hospital, I could see Angela was seriously ill. I stayed overnight at Mam's house. Angela went in to the operating theatre early the following morning. We got a phone call from the surgeon telling us to get to the hospital as soon as possible as Angela's condition had deteriorated. Angela had a burst aneurysm and there was nothing they could do about it. I could not imagine a world without Angela. For as long as I could remember Angela had been there. We had played our imaginary games together in the infant school, chasey's in the juniors. It was Angela and I who had gone to the Billingham International Folklore Festival. Enjoying the blaze of colour from the traditional costumes, eyeing up the young male dancers and choosing the ones we liked. Browsing round Binn's Department Store and other shops, looking for bargains. Angela and I had shared and supported each other through the difficult times. Things only Angela and I had known. We had fought like cats and dogs, we were chalk and cheese, but I loved her. Angela was not only my sister, she was my closest friend. Angela died on the Friday. She was only 42, 18 months older than me. The last thing Angela said before losing consciousness was, 'look after my kids'. Much of my time at the hospital was spent making arrangements for Angela's three children. Angela and I were very close, almost like twins. I still miss her very much and the only consolation I have is that she was a Christian. She is now with the Lord Jesus and one day I will see her again. I also lost my 18-year-old half-brother at the beginning of the year when he died following an epileptic fit. Throughout this time the Lord remained faithful.

My health improved greatly. I became part of the family, getting to know my children again. I cannot tell you how wonderful it is to take part in family life again, to sit in the same room, watch a programme with them, or play a game. Aaron discovered his mum could bake. I was able to go swimming and have one or two bike rides. Previously it had been an achievement just to walk my children to school. I have a new appreciation of everyday activities.

I started to read my bible again and set aside some time to be with the Lord. It is wonderful to see the Lord answering so many prayers. I attended a small house church, delighting in seeing our intercessory prayers answered.

During these years of testing, the Lord upheld me, Gus, and the children. I have learned, and am still learning, the valuable lesson of being still and knowing God. It is His faithfulness and love that have carried me through.

But those whose hope is in the Lord

Will renew their strength.
They will soar on wings like eagles:
They will run and not grow weary
They will walk and not be faint.
Isaiah 40:29-31

Happy Times

*"Praise Him on the trumpet, the psaltry
and harp, praise Him on the timbrel and
the dance.....
Let everything that has breath
praise the Lord"*

Psalm 150

2013, the year I turned fifty. Life was
good, I had lost two stone in weight, the
fittest I'd been in a long, long time. The
children were either away at university or
at college. There were fewer chores and
more time for each other. Fewer chores
meant that I could use my limited energy
to do things I enjoyed rather than things
that had to be done. I began gradually
building up the distance I could walk; Gus
and I would enjoy walking along the
beach front. We celebrated our 25th
wedding anniversary with a visit to
Berwick-upon-Tweed, taking a trip down
memory lane. We began ballroom dance
lessons in January. Before our first session
Gus said to me, 'If we learn enough to get
us round the dance floor I'll be satisfied'.

We were warmly welcomed right from the
start by our dance teacher's Michael and
Heather. After my experiences as a
teenager learning dance steps with Gillian,
I knew I had two left feet. Michael led us
onto the dance floor and showed us our
steps: '1,2, 3 and 1,2,3.' Three little steps,
that's all! It took all night (two hours, to
get it looking anything like a dance. After
we had succeeded doing 1,2, 3, 1,2,3
around the floor, Michael turned to us and
said, 'Those are all the steps you need to
get around the dance floor' We had
achieved our goal, but we were hooked!
There was so much more to learn. We
wanted to be graceful, light, and glide
across the floor, but we were far, far from
that! A few other couples started lessons
the same time as ourselves, and we have
become great friends both in and outside
of dancing.

There was going to be a dance weekend!
The ladies in our group, four of us, met
for coffee and lunch, discussing what we
were going to wear. There was to be a
1950's theme one night and the second
was to be a dinner dance with tuxedos and

evening dresses. We ladies decided we would be the Pink Ladies from Grease and persuade our men to dress accordingly. We went dress shopping. What fun we had trying on different evening dresses, getting each other's opinions. In the end I decided to have a go at making my own outfit. One of the ladies, Josie, was very skilled with the sewing machine and her enthusiasm rubbed off. For my Pink Lady outfit, I bought a lavender pink 50's dress with a wide circle skirt. I wore it with a black jacket, tights, and shoes, my hair was brushed into a beehive. Gus had skinny black jeans, a borrowed black leather jacket, white T-shirt, bright blue socks, and an Elvis style wig. When we entered the ballroom no one recognised us! For the formal evening I wore a dress I made with a great deal of help from friends. It was again in the 50's style, a tea length dress (I didn't want to trip up whilst dancing) of black satin, with a central panel of sequins in the skirt. It had a matching bolero. Gus and all the men looked very handsome in their tuxedos.

Never Let You Go

If we are faithless,
He will remain faithful
For He cannot disown Himself
2 Timothy

"Dad, you've got a droopy eye," observed
Ruth, now a junior doctor.
"It's been like that for ages," replied Gus.
It was Gus' birthday and we were all
gathered in the living room.
"Seriously Dad, it can be an indication of
a stroke or other serious illnesses."
We rolled our eyes, thinking Ruth was
over- reacting. However, Ruth wouldn't
let it go until we promised Gus would get
it checked out by the doctor.
The consultant told us there were three
possible causes, a loose piece of soft
tissue, Bell's Palsy or, more seriously, a
form of muscular dystrophy, a
degenerative disease. We had to wait
several weeks before we had the results of
tests.
What were we going to do! Gus was my
carer, I depended on him. Whatever the

outcome, I had to start doing more and not depend so much on him. I was going through the menopause, my sleep patterns were disturbed, I couldn't remember when I last had a good night's sleep. I woke each day more tired than the last. I had started to question my faith in God: did He really exist; how could I discern what Jesus was saying to me? Was it Him or just my own desires? My quiet times, when I had them, were difficult, my prayers seemed to hit the ceiling. I was unhappy, I thought our friends didn't really like me but only tolerated me because they liked Gus. At dancing we were mixing with friends who did exciting things, had jobs and careers, whilst my life was wasted at home, I was boring and had little to add. Even though the Lyme Disease was stabilized, I still struggled with energy levels and could not manage household tasks alone. Despite this, I determined to make an extra effort, even if it was just washing the dishes or doing the ironing. Gus' health threat made me realise that without him I could not manage our four-bedroom home. This was a good time to think about downsizing, a nice little bungalow perhaps. I began searching the property pages of the newspaper. One bungalow caught my eye. Three bedrooms, and on our estate, so not too much change. Three-bedroom bungalows rarely came up for sale on our estate, this must be the Lord's doing. I prayed about it and became convinced it was the one for us.

After a very long, stressful month, result day came. All tests were clear, it was just a loose piece of tissue which could be corrected with a small operation, or if it was not causing concern could be left as it is.

We were overjoyed, such a weight was lifted. Yet, it made me realise how vulnerable I was and I still wanted to downsize to make life easier. On the way home from hospital I shared these concerns with Gus. I shared about the bungalow. We drove past it and took a look. Gus agreed it was a good opportunity. Within the next few days we put our house on the market. I began sorting through our belongings, taking unwanted items to the local authority refuse tip, packing away the ones we wanted to keep. Frantically tidying the house ready for potential buyers. I exhausted myself yet I pushed on.

Walking past the Estate Agent's window I was devastated to see the bungalow had been sold. How could it be? I thought the Lord would save it for us. I was a failure. I no longer knew the Lord's voice; how could I have got it so wrong. We had lost our chance; it would be years before another bungalow would be available on this estate. Gus would not be happy to move further afield.

As we sat down to our Sunday lunch of roast chicken and Yorkshire puddings, Gus and I got into an argument. Upset, I stormed from the table and went to our bedroom.

I was so angry with *everything!* Angry with God for not giving us the bungalow. I was a complete waste of space. Life was such a struggle. I wanted to dance more, have more fun, but in order to spend an evening dancing, I had to spend the following week resting, as one evening, even if I only did three or four dances, would completely exhaust me. I tired of the restrictions this illness placed on me. I was a failure as a mother. The children did not have a close relationship with Jesus, they were living their own lives. I hadn't spent enough time with them as children, hadn't set them a good example. I'd failed my sister Angela, I wasn't good enough for God, He didn't want to use me on the mission field. Other family members who had once followed the Lord no longer did so. Perhaps I had been fooled all these years; God didn't exist, all I had lived for, had been for nothing. If there was no God then there was no hope, no reason to go on.

Something I had vowed never to do I now decided to do. However, if I was going to do it I would do it properly. Slipping quietly to the kitchen I topped my coffee up with liqueur. Back upstairs I took one pill after another. Every so often I thought, you haven't taken enough, take some more. I sent a text message to five people; it was a cryptic message only Gus would fully understand. Nobody replied. Nobody cares, I thought. They'll be better off without me; I wouldn't hold them back any more. Gus wouldn't have to look after me any more. Somewhere in my befuddled mind was a doubt, what if God does exist, if so you're going to hell. In desperation I cried out, 'Yeshua (Jesus), if you exist you will stop me doing this. Within *seconds* Gus came into the room.

'My phone was switched off in my pocket and it just switched itself on. I just read your text, what do you mean?'.

It didn't take him long to assess the situation. What happened next was a blur of Gus and the children talking, my being led into an ambulance. Lying on a hospital trolley, getting my bloods checked. I had got off lightly, Ruth told me later. I could have damaged major organs like kidneys and liver, my stomach could have ruptured, I could have been in a coma in a vegetative state. Looking at my children I saw the fear in their eyes, saw Aaron struggling to be a man. I knew what I was doing to them; I had been in the very same position as a child. I was empty. I had nothing to give. My initial thought was I had failed, I couldn't even do that properly. Once back at home, I was deeply ashamed, tired, and weepy. At the hospital they advised not to think about getting through the day, but to concentrate on getting through the next half hour. I clung to the fact Jesus had heard me and answered me. I had done something despicable yet He still loved me.

I had turned my back on Him, denied Him, but Jesus loved me. He held on to me, He didn't let me go. If there was no one else I could trust, I could trust Jesus. I lay in bed and played Don Francisco's song "I'll Never Let Go of Your Hand" over and over again.

I know what you've been hearing
I've seen you hide your fear
Embarrassed by your weaknesses
Afraid to let Me near
I wish you knew how much I long
For you to understand

No matter what may happen, child
I'll never let go of your hand

I know you've been forsaken
By all you've known before
When you've failed their expectations
They frown and close the door
But even though your heart itself
Should lose the will to stand
No matter what may happen, child
I'll never let go of your hand

The everlasting Father has
made His covenant with you
And He's stronger than the world
you've seen and heard So don't
you fear to show them All the love
I have for you I'll be with you
everywhere In everything you do
And even if you do it wrong And miss
the joy I planned I'll never, never
let go of your hand

The life that I have given you
No one can take away I've sealed
it with My Spirit, blood and word
The everlasting Father has

made His covenant with you
And He's stronger than
the world you've seen and heard
So don't you fear to show them
All the love I have for you
I'll be with you everywhere
In everything you do And even
if you do it wrong And miss
the joy I planned I'll never,
never let go of your hand
I'll never let go of your hand

I wept so many tears, deeply ashamed I begged for Jesus' forgiveness.

Recovery was extremely slow. I went for counselling and for the first time shared about my childhood, my grief for Angela, and my frustrations with having Lyme Disease. I was taught how to communicate my feelings in a more positive way. For the first time I could see how Mam had overdosed all those years ago. A single mother caring for four young girls, limited finances, no breaks or holidays, struggling with her own physical illness, she was completely exhausted, and she saw it as the only way she could make herself heard.

Jesus loved me, He was dependable, He is Lord of all, in control of all. When I turned my back on Him, when I was exposed to the powers of darkness, Jesus protected me. Nothing separated me from the Love of God in Christ Jesus. Without Jesus I am nothing, I am filthy, depraved, I have nothing to offer God. It is Jesus and His precious blood that makes the difference.

A New Creation

"Therefore, if anyone is in Christ,
he is a new creation."
                              2 Corinthians 5:17
"There is now no condemnation for
those who are in Christ."
                              Romans 8:1

Gradually, Jesus put my life back
together. I now know Jesus loves me, He
is showing me I am useful to Him, there
are things I can do. I started going to
Cameo group at church. Cameo meet once
a week; there are various activities one
can choose to get involved with. I joined
the art class. I have received compliments
for my work. After these activities a short
talk is given, then lunch is served. I help
with serving the lunches. The great thing
is I can turn up when I am able. There are
many there struggling with health
problems, so there is no pressure to turn
up every week. During my recovery I
began playing a fashion design game.
Within the game there are groups called
Fashion Houses, each group works

together to win prizes. I accidentally became leader of a Fashion House. The House has grown from four members who hardly won any prizes to almost 40 who win every prize. Members say the Fashion House is a special, friendly, and supportive place. I have learnt so much about myself: I can deal with difficult situations or players; I am good at making decisions and leading people. How can I use these gifts for God?

Jesus did not let me go. I am here for a reason; He has a job for me to do. I don't know what that is. I am still restricted by Lyme Disease, the battles are the same, but the difference is Jesus. I was called to serve Jesus many years ago. I have used children, illness, and all sorts of things as excuses for not doing His will. I repented of everything and offered myself to serve Jesus again. I told Him, 'I don't know what I can do, or how you can use me, but I want to live fully for you again.' The Lord is working in both mine and Gus' life. For the first time in years we are studying the scriptures and praying together. We have given all our activities, everything we do to Him, asking Him to

show us what is to stay and what is to go,
and where does God want us.

I don't know what the future holds but

> *"I know Whom I have believed,*
> *And am persuaded that He is able*
> *To keep that which I've committed*
> *Unto Him against that day."*
> Daniel W Whittle 1883

If you enjoyed reading this book please leave a review on the site from which it was purchased/read.

Printed in Great Britain
by Amazon

20994206R00082